Living Through a
NATURAL
DISASTER

By Eve Recht

Series Literacy Consultant
Dr Ros Fisher

Pearson Education Limited
Edinburgh Gate
Harlow
Essex CM20 2JE
England

www.longman.co.uk

ISBN 0 582 84124 0

Colour reproduction by Colourscan, Singapore
Printed and bound in China by Leo Paper Products Ltd.

The Publisher's policy is to use paper manufactured from sustainable forests.

The following people from **DK** have
contributed to the development of this product:

Art Director Rachael Foster

Martin Wilson **Managing Art Editor** | **Managing Editor** Marie Greenwood
Kath Northam **Design** | **Editorial** Hannah Wilson
Cynthia Frazer **Picture Research** | **Production** Gordana Simakovic
Richard Czapnik, Andy Smith **Cover Design** | **DTP** David McDonald
Consultant Keith Lye

Dorling Kindersley would like to thank: Northern Territory Library and Information Services, Australia, for Cyclone Tracy witness accounts;
David Ferguson for additional consultancy; Rose Horridge in the DK Picture Library; Ed Merrit for cartography;
and Johnny Pau for additional cover design work.

Picture Credits: Chinapix: 5c, 13b, 17t, 18–19, 19tl, 19tr, 20. Corbis: 5t; Yann Arthus-Bertrand 12b; Bettmann 6b; Gary Braasch 22b; Jay Dickman
23t; Wolfgang Kaehler 16; Nasa 7cr; Jose Luis Pelaez, Inc 7–8t, 32; Carl and Ann Purcell 27b; Arthur Rothstein 29c; Vince Streano 1; John Maier
Jr/Argus Fotoarchiv/Sygma 26; Richard Ellis/Sygma 24b; Julia Waterlow/Eye Ubiquitous 14–15. FLPA - Images of nature: 9, 10bl; Ray Bird 3. Getty
Images: Agence FP 22t; Paul and Lindamarie Ambrose 4–5; Yoav Lemmer/AFP 29b. Hutchison Library: Michael Kahn 24t; Liba Taylor 27t. Katz/FSP:
Wayne Miles 12t. Northern Territory Library, Australia: Robert Wesley-Smith Collection 10cr, 10br. Popperfoto: 11; AFP 29t; Daniel LeClair/Reuters
25; Rafiqur Rahman/Reuters 30l; Reuters 17b; Steve Wood/Royal Navy/Reuters 30r. Reuters: Jorge Silva 5b, 21b. Topfoto: Image Works 28.
Cover: Corbis: Jose Luis Pelaez, Inc. front t; Vince Streano back. Popperfoto: AFP front bl.

All other images: DK Dorling Kindersley © 2004. For further information see www.dkimages.com
Dorling Kindersley Ltd., 80 Strand, London WC2R ORL

Contents

Extreme Weather

For most people the weather is not particularly surprising. There are rainy days or clear skies. Some days are warm and some days are cold. However, in some parts of the world the weather is very dangerous. Some places have incredibly powerful winds and torrential rain. Other places have no rain for months and months.

If bad weather is forecasted, then people can prepare for it. However, this isn't always possible. Sometimes bad weather arrives unexpectedly and kills many people.

A tropical cyclone almost destroyed an Australian city in 1974.

Severe floods brought death and hardship to many thousands of Chinese in 1933.

Drought brought disaster to several Central American countries in 1997 and 1998.

Tropical cyclones, or hurricanes, are one of the most extreme storms people experience. These storms build over the oceans in the tropics, close to the equator. If they strike a coastline, then they may cause a great deal of damage. In late 1974 Tracy, a small but severe cyclone hit the city of Darwin, Australia. It became the worst natural disaster that any Australian city had ever experienced.

Many people who live beside rivers worry about extreme rainfall. Too much rain causes water levels to rise and spill over the riverbanks, flooding farmland and homes. In 1933 the Huang He River in China, flooded. It had devastating consequences.

Drought is just as extreme as cyclones and floods. In a drought, rain may not fall for months or years. As plants and animals die from lack of water, many people starve. In 1997 a severe drought affected many people in Central America.

The Story of Cyclone Tracy

South East Asia

Equator

Darwin

PACIFIC OCEAN

Australia

N
W E
S

Canberra

On 24th December 1974 the residents of Darwin in Australia, were enjoying the summer. It was Christmas Eve, and many people were celebrating. At about 9:30 pm, the weather service broadcasted cyclone warnings. Most people were too busy preparing for Christmas Day to pay much attention to the warnings. Then, just after midnight, the cyclone hit Darwin with heavy rain and winds of more than 200 kilometres per hour.

By the next morning, Darwin had been devastated. Most buildings were flattened, and there was no power. Trucks and planes had been blown around like toys. During Cyclone Tracy's night of destruction in Darwin, more than sixty people were killed, and hundreds had been injured.

Tracy left the city of Darwin in ruins.

What Is a Cyclone?

Tropical cyclones are powerful storm systems that develop over warm ocean waters. In North America, these storms are called hurricanes, whereas in Australia they are called cyclones. In eastern Asia, they are known as typhoons. A tropical cyclone develops when warm, moist air is sucked into an area of low pressure. Over time, huge thunderclouds build up and strong winds begin to rotate around the storm centre.

A Night of Destruction

Like many other Darwin residents, Bob Collins didn't pay too much attention to the cyclone warnings on 24th December. In the evening he was at his home just outside the city. Bob described the dramatic events of the night that followed in this way:

❯❯ At about midnight, it was clear that this was going to be something significant and scary. The wind just kept on getting stronger and stronger. It went past the point where you'd ever experienced anything like it before ...

And then, in the early hours of the morning ... there was this enormous sort of ripping, tearing sound and in a matter of seconds, the entire roof just peeled off the house ... It sucked the ceilings out ... And we were just surrounded by the brick walls of the house, with rain and wind just shooting into the house. It was absolutely terrifying. ❯❯

Bob Collins and his friends drove to his office building which was "cyclone-proof". A cyclone-proof building is usually constructed with steel and concrete. Bob described the difficult trip to his office:

> \\ The three of us jammed ourselves into this four-wheel drive and took off ... in the eye of the storm. There was of course this artificial lull. And the sight that I saw in the headlights of the vehicle ... was just extraordinary. Trees laying ... across the road.... [Then] the storm had actually come back the other way ... We were very lucky to make it. //

The "Eye"

The area of calm in the middle of a cyclone is called the eye. It is surrounded by a wall of thick clouds, driving rains and spiralling winds. When the eye of the storm is directly overhead, the winds suddenly drop and the sky clears for a short time (usually an hour or two). After the eye has passed, the fierce winds and rain start again, but this time they blow from the opposite direction.

layers of spiralling winds

eye

wall

Cyclone cross-section

Not many of Darwin's residents ventured out into the cyclone. Rob Wesley-Smith stayed in his flat. He told the story of his struggle to save his photographs and personal papers in this way:

> \\ The suction ... was just unbelievable. I couldn't stop things blowing out. I tried to shut the door ... but the building must have been moving and the thing just swung open ... I'd gone to bed ... and woke up with a cyclone raging. //

A Morning of Devastation

On the morning of 25th December 1974 the residents of Darwin emerged from their safe places to face the destruction of their city. What they saw was shocking. Some people described the scene as looking like a battlefield. Others said the city had been turned into a huge rubbish dump.

That morning, Bob Collins drove to the ambulance station to see if he could help anyone. He described the scene around the city:

> \\ Seeing those big, high-tension power lines, the actual steel poles that held them up, twisted like liquorice ... I went past the old Darwin airport ... Millions of dollars worth, literally, of aircraft had just been blown up in a heap like ... garbage. //

Coping With the Chaos

The police began cleaning up early in the morning. Service people from the army, navy, and air force joined them on December 26. They brought along specialized equipment, such as electricity generators, to help restore utilities. Doctors and nurses arrived to treat people who were injured or in shock. They brought basic supplies, such as food, blankets, and tents that would provide temporary shelter for those who had been left homeless.

Bob Collins, one of many ordinary residents who volunteered to help, described how the streets were cleared:

> **❚❚** Graders and bulldozers [were] out on the roads, and they'd actually graded tracks through the debris, and moved bits of houses and sheet iron and broken glass that was everywhere. **❚❚**

Rob Wesley-Smith took these two photos of a ruined building and trees stripped of their leaves.

This photo shows two cars that had been picked up by the winds and dropped into a nearby swimming pool.

Thousands of people had lost nearly everything they owned. Houses were destroyed and their contents blown away or soaked with rain and mud. It was difficult to look for things in the mess of rubble, uprooted trees, and mangled cars. The city was in ruins, and the government's emergency team decided to evacuate everyone as soon as possible.

Darwin's population when Tracy hit was about 44,000. By December 31, only about 11,000 people remained. About 26,000 people left by air and more than 7,000 by road. Many people did not return to Darwin for several years. Others never returned.

Dawn Lawrie described the strange evacuation scene:

> **\\ The evacuation was a once in a lifetime experience.... It was a mass evacuation ... [but] there was quite a stillness and a quietness. I worked assisting them [the people] to get to the plane.... We crammed the people on. I think we hold the world record for getting numbers of actual people in the aircraft. //**

Darwin Today

During the next thirty years, Darwin was rebuilt. Strict regulations were introduced to ensure that all new buildings could withstand the force of a cyclone. Some buildings were built to allow winds to blow through them, leaving the main structure standing. Others used reinforcing steel rods to fix them firmly to the ground. Public cyclone shelters were also built.

Cyclones are most likely to occur during the wet season which runs from October to March. During this period the people of Darwin are on their guard. Hopefully, they will be better prepared should another disastrous visitor like Cyclone Tracy arrive.

All new buildings erected in Darwin – even those delivered by truck – are cyclone-proof.

Today Darwin has been rebuilt and is an active city again.

The Huang He Flood

The Huang He winds its way down from the mountainous region in the heart of China. It then meanders eastwards across the vast North China Plain before emptying into the Yellow Sea.

Often the lower section of the river floods the flat plains, making that region a dangerous place to live. However, flooding brings riches as well as disaster. A layer of silt is left by the floods which makes the plains fertile. The crops grown there feed millions of people.

In 1933 the Huang He flooded. It swept through towns, villages and farmland. It killed thousands of people and left millions homeless.

People fled from the flood by boat.

The Yellow River

Huang He means "yellow river" in Chinese. It is called this because tonnes of yellow-coloured silt collects on its journey and turns the river yellow. This silt is very fertile so it nourishes the surrounding land when the river floods.

Silt settles on the riverbed, and as it builds up, the water level rises. In times of heavy rain, the river overflows its banks, flooding the region.

For hundreds of years, the people who lived along the Huang He tried to find ways to control the frequent river floods. They dug out the silt and built canals to direct the water elsewhere. However, the silt continued to cause the level of the riverbed to rise. Over the years, the higher riverbed raised the level of the water in the river. In some places, the water flowed along a riverbed of mud that was more than 4.5 metres above the level of the surrounding plains.

Finally the people decided that the best way to stop the river from overflowing was to build up the banks of the river to form high walls called dikes. Unfortunately, this only made the situation worse.

This is the muddy, yellow Huang He today. At about 4,800 metres long, it is one of the world's longest rivers.

Heavy Rain

The rainy season in central China occurs every June and July. In June 1933 the farmers strengthened the dikes as they did each year. However, the rains in July were so heavy that the water overflowed the dikes in some places. People worked as fast as they could to build the dikes higher.

How the Huang He Became So High

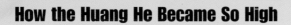

silt piles up on riverbed

river overflows its banks

1 Silt collected on the riverbed, pushing up the water level. During heavy rain, the water spilled over the banks.

dike

river contained within dikes

2 Farmers built dikes along the riverbanks. The dikes usually stopped the water from flowing out onto surrounding fields.

water level rises

dike raised

silt builds up

3 As more silt built up, the water kept rising. Farmers built the dikes higher, and the water level got dangerously high.

As the weeks passed, the rains kept falling and the river level continued to rise. A huge amount of water now flowed along its high riverbed above the farmland, villages and towns on the plains.

The swiftly moving water pounded the walls of the dikes until they could no longer take it. The dikes began to break. People frantically tried to repair the gaps by plugging them with bundles of kaoliang stalks, rocks and earth. But the rushing water kept pulling away more and more material from the dikes, making the gaps even wider.

Today the dikes along many of China's rivers are reinforced with a crisscross of steel pipes.

Kaoliang

In the past, dikes were made mainly of bundles of kaoliang stalks: a grain that grows on the North China Plain. Kaoliang, which is also called Chinese sorghum, has been an important building material and food crop in China for thousands of years. Its seeds, or grain, are used for animal feed.

kaoliang   calabash   maize

Chinese crops

The Huang He Overflows

Many of the river dikes collapsed without warning. Water rushed through the enormous cracks. The entire river emptied onto the plains, creating a huge flood of muddy, swirling water.

People fled for their lives, but thousands drowned in the massive waterfalls that poured down from the high banks of the river. Some people survived by climbing trees and rooftops. They waited in these high places, enduring hunger, thirst and the pouring rain, hoping to be rescued.

Other people fled by boat. They gathered whatever possessions they could and desperately paddled away from the flooded areas. As they escaped, they tried to rescue anyone who was stranded.

Waters of the Huang He flooded about 11,600 square kilometres of farmland, villages and towns.

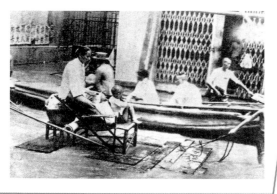

In the towns, streets became rivers along which people fled in flat-bottomed boats called sampans.

After the floodwaters retreated, the homes left standing were buried under thick mud. More than three million people were left homeless and had to dig in the mud to find scraps of material to rebuild their houses. All the crops on the plains were ruined, so thousands of people starved.

The Huang He Today

To prepare for future floods, trees and other vegetation were planted along the river. Plants help to absorb rainfall and to reduce soil erosion that washes silt into the river.

However, many people who live along the Huang He are faced with a different problem today. After decades of drought, deforestation and mismanagement, some parts of the Huang He are nearly dry. Since local people, farms and industries rely on the river for their water supply, this situation is causing huge problems. Du Paiyuan is the manager of a copper factory in the city of Taiyun. He explained how the lack of water was affecting his workers:

> \\ Some of our employees have had no water for days. They can't clean their homes ... They can only take showers once a week. //

To deal with the low water levels, wells are being dug. Canals could also bring water to the Huang He from the Chang Jiang (Yangtze River). However, this project would be very expensive and may not provide the water needed.

Today some parts of the Huang He are almost dry.

El Niño Brings Drought

El Niño is a pattern of winds and ocean currents that affects the Earth's weather. In different parts of the world it can trigger storms, floods or drought at the same time.

In 1997 and 1998 El Niño produced a terrible drought in much of Central America. Crops and farm animals died, and forest fires raged across the parched land. Food and water shortages affected almost one million people.

This Guatemalan farmer's crops were destroyed by El Niño-related drought.

An Unstable Environment

Central America is made up of
Guatemala, Belize, El Salvador,
Honduras, Nicaragua, Costa Rica and
Panama. These countries have a diverse
range of plants and animals. There are
tropical rainforests, swamps, beaches
and mountains. It is an important
agricultural area, and many of its
residents make a living producing
coffee, sugar and maize.

In October 1998, soon after the
drought ended, Hurricane Mitch
brought floods to Honduras
(above) and to Nicaragua.

Unfortunately, the rich and varied environment
has suffered over the years. It lies in an unstable
part of the Earth and is prone to earthquakes
and volcanic eruptions. It has also been hit
by many hurricanes.

Human activities have threatened Central
America's environment, too. Rainforests have
been cut down, destroying the habitats of
many animals and weakening the ability
of the soil to support plants and trees.

In Costa Rica, rainforests
have been cut down
or burnt to clear land
for farming.

El Niño probably has the greatest effect on Central America's ecosystem. The region needs to receive a certain quantity of water each month to maintain its crops and supply water to its people.

During El Niño, which occurs about every two to seven years, Central America receives little or no rain at all for several months. Other regions are also affected by El Niño. During 1997–1998 the Philippines, Australia and Indonesia experienced drought caused by El Niño. At the same time, floods occurred in Peru and Ecuador in South America.

El Niño of 1997–1998 brought heavy rain to Peru.

El Niño and Ocean Currents

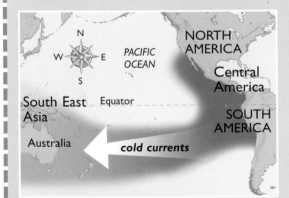

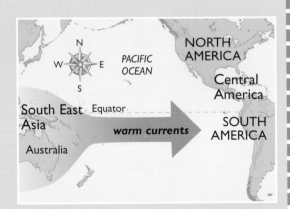

Normal conditions
Most of the time, westerly winds produce ocean currents that carry cool surface waters away from South America towards Australia. This effect brings heavy rainfall to South East Asia while cold ocean water rises up along the coast of South America.

El Niño conditions
During El Niño, the westerly winds die down and change direction. Surface currents are reversed. They now carry warm ocean water in an easterly direction across the Pacific Ocean. This change has a dramatic effect on rainfall patterns worldwide.

An Unexpected El Niño

In May 1997 the waters in the Pacific Ocean had already warmed up by 2°C in places. Also, storm systems normally found over Indonesia were moving East. Both of these changes indicated that a new El Niño was beginning.

In most cases, meteorologists can predict El Niño up to a year in advance. However, the scientists didn't realize the 1997 El Niño was under way until six months before the warm water arrived off the coast of South America.

David Parker is an El Niño tracker at Britain's Meteorological Office. He predicted that the 1997 El Niño would have devastating effects. He was correct. This is what he said:

Meteorologists study data about Earth's atmosphere to learn about the weather.

❯❯ The consequences [of El Niño] will probably be felt worldwide over the coming year ... So far, 1997 is already the second warmest year ever, so we could see a new record. ❯❯

Studying El Niño

This satellite photograph shows the warm El Niño current in the Pacific in June 1997. Meteorologists use images like this to help them understand El Niño. Although they know when an El Niño weather pattern is starting to form, they still do not know why the ocean currents change direction.

warm El Niño current

Central America

Australia

Pacific Ocean

Devastation

For many months at the end of 1997 and the beginning of 1998, most of Central America was devastated by drought. Crops withered under the hot, dry conditions and the intense heat caused roads to buckle. Rivers and lakes dried up, and the water levels in reservoirs steadily dropped. Some people died from starvation during the drought, and many died from the heat.

Both rural and urban areas were affected. Farmers watched their crops fail, and together with the city dwellers, they suffered food and water shortages.

A farmer in Honduras surveys his withered maize crop.

This dry weather shrivelled trees and other plants, creating conditions perfect for wildfires. As forests burned, animal habitats were destroyed. Many people who worked gathering and selling forest products lost their jobs. Smoke from fires made breathing difficult for people and animals. For months, the skies were polluted by a grey haze of smoke that caused health problems and poor visibility.

Coping With the Disaster

Most countries in Central America were not prepared for the devastating effects of the drought. As harvests failed, people starved. Some countries were helped by international aid agencies. Emergency food supplies were shipped to the worst areas. However, the longer the drought continued, the more severe the disaster became.

In Guatemala and other countries in Central America, emergency food supplies were handed out.

Other countries, such as Costa Rica, did not request international help. Instead they acted immediately at the beginning of the drought. First they declared a "state of emergency", so water and transport could be controlled. Water was limited so that none was wasted. Wells were built around the country to gain access to more underground water. Throughout the crisis, the people were informed about El Niño and its effects.

In some countries in Central America, including Costa Rica, cattle were herded away from the driest areas.

Central America Today

Costa Rica's actions worked. By May 1998 the country had survived the crisis. They had produced a plan to allow people to have food and water throughout the drought and to limit damage to livestock and crops. They would know what to do when El Niño and drought returned.

In recent years, drought has returned to Central America frequently, and each time, emergency aid programmes have been put in place. In a region that is constantly battered by hurricanes, floods, earthquakes and drought, long-term planning is necessary to help the people and their land survive.

The beaches of Costa Rica attract tourism, bringing much-needed money into the country.

Handling Natural Disasters

Cyclone Tracy, the Huang He flood and the drought in Central America all caused major population changes. Cyclone Tracy caused the evacuation of three-quarters of Darwin's population. The 1933 flood in China caused the temporary relocation of millions of citizens. Central America's drought in 1997–1998 forced many people to move to areas with more water.

Natural disasters affect huge groups of people, either directly or indirectly. They bring death, famine, disease and homelessness. They destroy landscapes, wiping out crops and cattle.

It is important to learn how to deal with natural disasters. In this final section read how international aid organizations provide support to areas hit by disaster. Learn how meteorologists and other scientists work towards a greater understanding of the Earth and its weather systems, too.

Other Floods, Droughts and Tropical Cyclones

One of the most deadly cyclones on record occurred in Bangladesh on 30th April 1991. More than 139,000 people died.

For seven years in the 1930s the United States suffered a severe drought. It destroyed huge areas of farmland.

In February 2000 heavy rain in southern Africa caused terrible floods in Mozambique. More than one million people had to leave their homes.

International Aid Organizations

International disaster-relief agencies help people all over the world who have been affected by severe storms, floods and drought. For example, the Red Cross and the Red Crescent provide emergency aid when disaster strikes. They supply food, water, clothing and medicine. They also provide shelter (often tents), for those who have been left homeless.

One of the main roles of relief agencies is to offer comfort and emotional support to people who have been traumatized by natural disaster. Like many relief organizations, the Red Cross and the Red Crescent also set up long-term programmes. Volunteers spend months, or even years, in countries that need their help. They provide equipment and advice for local people so they can help themselves after the aid organizations have left.

A Red Crescent volunteer gives a bag of relief goods to a young victim of flooding in Bangladesh.

A Red Cross worker holds a baby girl in Honduras after Hurricane Mitch struck in 1998.

Understanding the Earth

Meteorologists and other scientists carefully study tropical storms, floods, droughts and other natural disasters to learn as much as they can about our planet. They examine data and photographs provided by satellites. They search for patterns in weather systems and changes to the Earth's climate. They use special equipment to monitor changes that could indicate that a disaster is about to occur.

This information is vital to people who live in dangerous areas. They hope that scientists will be able to predict where, when and how severe a cyclone or flood will be. With detailed warnings, people can try to limit the consequences of natural disasters.

Climate Change

Climate change is a change in the Earth's long-term weather patterns. Presently, the Earth is experiencing a warming trend. When fossil fuels – coal, oil and gas – are burned, carbon dioxide gas is released into the atmosphere. Carbon dioxide traps heat and holds it near the Earth's surface. In recent years, this "global warming" has caused the ice caps at the poles to begin to melt. This results in raised sea levels and a change in ocean currents and rainfall patterns.

Scientists predict that due to global warming, El Niño will be more frequent, resulting in more severe weather conditions. Cutting down on the use of fossil fuels and avoiding pollution of the atmosphere will help to prevent global warming.

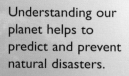

Understanding our planet helps to predict and prevent natural disasters.

Index